CQ/CX

Gabe McKinley

A Samuel French Acting Edition

FOUNDED 1830

SAMUELFRENCH.COM
SAMUELFRENCH-LONDON.CO.UK

Copyright © 2014 by Gabe McKinley
All Rights Reserved

CQ/CX is fully protected under the copyright laws of the United States of America, the British Commonwealth, including Canada, and all other countries of the Copyright Union. All rights, including professional and amateur stage productions, recitation, lecturing, public reading, motion picture, radio broadcasting, television and the rights of translation into foreign languages are strictly reserved.

ISBN 978-0-573-70170-2

www.SamuelFrench.com
www.SamuelFrench-London.co.uk

For Production Enquiries

United States and Canada
Info@SamuelFrench.com
1-866-598-8449

United Kingdom and Europe
Theatre@SamuelFrench-London.co.uk
020-7255-4302

Each title is subject to availability from Samuel French, depending upon country of performance. Please be aware that *CQ/CX* may not be licensed by Samuel French in your territory. Professional and amateur producers should contact the nearest Samuel French office or licensing partner to verify availability.

CAUTION: Professional and amateur producers are hereby warned that *CQ/CX* is subject to a licensing fee. Publication of this play(s) does not imply availability for performance. Both amateurs and professionals considering a production are strongly advised to apply to Samuel French before starting rehearsals, advertising, or booking a theatre. A licensing fee must be paid whether the title(s) is presented for charity or gain and whether or not admission is charged. Professional/Stock licensing fees are quoted upon application to Samuel French.

No one shall make any changes in this title(s) for the purpose of production. No part of this book may be reproduced, stored in a retrieval system, or transmitted in any form, by any means, now known or yet to be invented, including mechanical, electronic, photocopying, recording, videotaping, or otherwise, without the prior written permission of the publisher. No one shall upload this title(s), or part of this title(s), to any social media websites.

For all enquiries regarding motion picture, television, and other media rights, please contact Samuel French.

MUSIC USE NOTE

Licensees are solely responsible for obtaining formal written permission from copyright owners to use copyrighted music in the performance of this play and are strongly cautioned to do so. If no such permission is obtained by the licensee, then the licensee must use only original music that the licensee owns and controls. Licensees are solely responsible and liable for all music clearances and shall indemnify the copyright owners of the play(s) and their licensing agent, Samuel French, against any costs, expenses, losses and liabilities arising from the use of music by licensees. Please contact the appropriate music licensing authority in your territory for the rights to any incidental music.

IMPORTANT BILLING AND CREDIT REQUIREMENTS

If you have obtained performance rights to this title, please refer to your licensing agreement for important billing and credit requirements.

CQ/CX was first produced by the Atlantic Theater Company at the Peter Norton Space on January 25, 2012 in New York City. The performance was directed by David Leveaux, with sets by David Rockwell costumes by Jess Goldstein, lighting by Ben Stanton, sound by David Van Tieghem, and projections by Peter Nigrini and C. Andrew Bauer. The Production Stage Manager was Jenna Woods. The cast was as follows:

JAY BENNETT	Kobi Libii
JACOB SHERMAN	Steve Rosen
MONICA SORIA	Sheila Tapia
HAL MARTIN	Arliss Howard
GEARALD HAYNES	Peter Jay Fernandez
JUNIOR	David Pittu
FRANK KING	Larry Bryggman
BEN	Tim Hopper

CHARACTERS

JAY BENNETT – Reporter, African American, early 20s
JACOB SHERMAN – Reporter, Jewish, 20s
MONICA SORIA – Reporter, 20s
HAL MARTIN – Executive Editor, 50s
GEARALD HAYNES – Editor, African American, 50s
JUNIOR – Publisher, Jewish, late 40s
FRANK KING – Editor, 60s
BEN – Editor, 50s

ACT I

1

(A dark conference room at The New York Times.)

(A slide show is going on. Out of the darkness a picture is projected before the audience.)

(First slide: A picture of a young black woman, she gazes off into the distance.)

*(A man's voice, **JUNIOR**, narrates the slide show.)*

VOICE. How do you identify a story?

(a click)

(Second slide: The same picture of the woman, but not cropped, it shows the woman in a soup line, she gazes at food being slopped on a plate.)

(a click)

(Third slide: A hole in the ground, obviously caused by an explosion.)

What is its context?

(a click)

(Fourth slide: The same picture of the hole, only not cropped. We see a baby's tattered shoe next to the hole.)

How does a story change?

(a click)

(Fifth slide: a photo of a child, a little girl, crying. The child reaches out for something unseen.)

(a click)

(Sixth Slide: The same photo of the crying baby girl, now it is revealed that she reaches for her father, who is taken away in handcuffs.)

(The lights come up to reveal a conference room at the Times. **JUNIOR**, *the publisher, speaks out to some seen or unseen fresh faced young reporters, this is the incoming group of interns.)*

*(***JUNIOR**, *a bookish man in his 40s, looks younger than he is, but is betrayed by a few gray hairs. Born rich and smart,* **JUNIOR** *has a schoolboy charm and a self-effacing manner.)*

JUNIOR. What these pictures should illustrate is the importance of a comprehensive view toward the gathering and reporting of news here at the paper. They're mnemonic devices reminding you to always take the time to look at the whole picture, because, as cliche as it sounds, there is always another side to the story. Also, no such thing as an easy answer and there is always another question to ask, another phone call to make…and don't worry about the phone bill, because I'll pay it… I'm good for it. *(laughing at his own joke)* My father began this program in 1984 when he was publisher. It was one of his great passions, he originally established it for members of minority groups who had been historically excluded from opportunities in America's newspaper industry. The program is open to everybody now, but remains an integral part of the our commitment to recruit and hire as diverse and as highly qualified a staff as possible. We think we've accomplished these goals with this remarkable group of interns. Ten young journalist. Just ten of you, chosen from hundreds of applicants, to make up the 1998 Reston, Rosenbaum and Morgan fellows.

*(***JUNIOR** *applauds them.)*

Now, that'll officially be the last time you are ever called fellows here in the newsroom. More often than not you will be called interns or more probably, "hey kid"…or "hand me that," or my favorite, "where is my copy?" Or any number of far less glamorous nomenclature. Now...*now* the real work begins. You're each going to be assigned to different desks and departments where you'll be expected to learn and more importantly *produce*. We have three hundred and seventy-five staff writers, four hundred editors and over four hundred other news designers and clerks working in our various newsrooms and bureaus. We have sixteen bureaus in New York State, eleven national news bureaus, twenty-five foreign news bureaus. The paper has been awarded over eighty Pulitzer Prizes in journalism...and now we have...you. We are the first thing the President of the United States reads every morning. At the end of this internship, some of you will be asked to return as intermediate reporters...some of you won't. But, right now, you have an opportunity. My family has been publishing this paper since 1896, so this is more than a business, it is more than a newspaper...it's a legacy. Welcome to the The New York Times. Welcome you to my family.

(The sounds of presses running, motion, speed pulsing into...)

2

(Office sounds. The newsroom of the Times. *Editors hunched over computers.)*

*(***BEN***, the Metro Desk editor, stares intently at his screen. He speaks to an unseen* **CLERK***.)*

BEN. Can you get me Jay Bennett?

GERALD. *(off stage)* Ben? Where's Ben?

(A short moment passes and **GERALD** *Haynes approaches* **BEN***'s desk. He is confident and urgent.)*

*(***GERALD***, a sturdy black man in his 50s.* **GERALD** *is the first black member of the* Times *masthead, its top editors; a hard fought victory. On first impression,* **GERALD** *is an intimidating presence. Large in stature, he oozes an authority won, in part, by a contained rage. Despite this,* **GERALD** *is most disarming when he smiles, which isn't often.)*

Ben, can we talk.

BEN. It's not a good time, Gerald.

GERALD. Can we make it a good time?

BEN. What's this about?

GERALD. What do you think it's about?

BEN. I know...you want David for the series on race, but I can't spare him.

GERALD. It's one essay, Ben.

BEN. Yeah. Two thousand words. Travel. I'd have to detach him, and I can't afford to. I need him for the daily...it comes out, ya know, every day.

GERALD. He wants to write it.

BEN. I need him. Wait, he told you he wants write something? Do me a favor and go through me, Gerald.

GERALD. I don't have to, Ben.

CLERK. *(off stage)* Bennett on one.

BEN. *(to* **GERALD***)* Can this wait?

GERALD. No.

BEN. You can't have David. He is one of my best writers and it's my call. I have state budget gridlock and a possible transit strike and…

GERALD. You're not going to scuttle this series.

BEN. And you're not going to scuttle the metro desk for some… *(stopping himself)* I don't want to scuttle your series. Now, I gotta go…

(BEN looks at his phone.)

(to CLERK)

There is nobody on one.

GERALD. For some…what? What are your thoughts on the race series, Ben? Not a big enough issue for you?

BEN. Give me a break, I have the page one meeting…

GERALD. How would you describe the race expose?

BEN. As a vanity project. Okay?

(to CLERK)

Can you get me Bennett again?

GERALD. I know we had our differences in Washington.

BEN. This has nothing to do with Washington. It has to do with the fact that I need David here, where he works. Find another writer.

(JAY, 20s, African American, arrives at BEN's desk, oblivious to the rising tension.)

JAY. You needed me?

BEN. Just a sec… I'm sorry, Gerald.

GERALD. This is personal.

BEN. It would make it so much easier if it was, wouldn't it? It's numbers. You know that. You had this same job…

JAY. I'll come back.

BEN. Just wait.

GERALD. It was a courtesy, that I even asked permission.

BEN. Then go to Joe. Ask him. But you know how I feel and where I stand.

GERALD. This isn't over.

*(**GERALD** storms away. **BEN**, oblivious, is back to his computer.)*

BEN. I'm sorry about that Jeff.

JAY. Jay.

BEN. I was reading your summary of the mall story. It's…

JAY. What?

BEN. This is good. The quote from the deputy mayor is fantastic. "It's a real long shot to think that tourists would choose Elizabeth, N.J., over Manhattan," Deputy Mayor Randy Levine said. "I mean, who gets on a plane and says, 'Honey, let's go fly to Elizabeth." *(beat)* That's a good quote, Jay…very good quote. They should give you an editor's award just for getting the deputy mayor on the phone after three on a Friday.

JAY. I checked on Alta Vista and was able to find his personal cell number on a contact list for his kid's school.

BEN. Alta Vista?

JAY. The search engine…the…internet.

BEN. That information is on the web?

JAY. You just have to know where to look.

BEN. Hm. Nothing better than a little New York versus New Jersey story. We sure this Jersey mall is bigger than the mall in Minnesota? Doesn't that one have a roller coaster in it?

JAY. I'm waiting on a call from this… *(checking his notes)* …International Council of Shopping Centers on the actual figures.

BEN. Can you email me the lede for the page one meeting? I'm gonna offer it. Joe loves this stuff. Okay. Get to work. You got to finish the story if you want us to publish it. Get out of here.

CLERK. *(off stage)* Who is Jay Bennett? We have a call.

JAY. Right here. Extension 7071. Two seconds.

BEN. Send me the top of your story right *now*.

(JAY runs off to catch the call. BEN stares at his screen, to his papers, preparing to leave for a meeting.)

(BEN stands shouting to unseen editors.)

Is this the right version of the shooting story in Backfield? It looks old. I don't know, it says you were the last to touch it. I didn't. So it's good? I'm gonna offer SHOOT, SLAY and MALL. The intern, Bennett, wrote it. He is sending me the top right now.

CLERK. *(off stage)* Gerald Haynes on one.

(BEN answers.)

BEN. Gerald, ya know, I've thought it over and I've decided…I'm not going to let you have David for the race series. Can I put you on hold?

(BEN slams the phone down, hanging up on GERALD. BEN picks up the phone and dials.)

Jay, it's Ben. That hasn't landed yet. I need that…

(BEN hangs up and is getting ready to leave, when JAY returns.)

JAY. Ben…

BEN. Did you send that? I need that, I'm late for the meeting.

(to CLERK)

Are you printing the ledes?

JAY. I just got off the phone with that council, and they are disputing the developers' numbers. They say that the square footage of the mall only makes it the sixth largest in the state of New Jersey.

BEN. Okay then. I gotta run.

JAY. So you're not going to offer it for page one?

BEN. The sixth largest mall in New Jersey is not a page one story…not even in a Saturday paper. Give me four hundred great words, and we'll get it in the city edition.

JAY. Four hundred? Wait.

BEN. That's the way it is… It's the facts of the story. You did good work. That was just a correction waiting to happen.

JAY. Is there another angle, maybe?

BEN. Did you CQ it?

JAY. CQ?

BEN. Cadit Quaestio. The question falls. The facts have been checked. Sometimes the sixth largest mall in New Jersey is just the sixth largest mall in New Jersey.

(**BEN** *walks away, stops, returns.*)

That's a great quote. I'll make sure to offer it as quote of the day. Page two. It's a hell of a lot closer than page B13, which is where the story is going to end up. And…Jay?

JAY. Yeah.

BEN. It's an office, and the Times. Could you wear something a little more appropriate to work?

(**BEN**, *with little regard, exits.* **JAY** *lingers in the distance.*)

CLERK. *(off stage)* Ben, Gerald on one. Ben, Gerald Haynes is on line one.

3

(Smith's Bar. The class of interns, now intermediate reporters, drink and talk.)

*(***MONICA*** Soria, 20s, a Texas girl of Mexican descent.)*

*(***JACOB*** Sherman, 20s, a New York native.)*

*(Nearby, ***FRANK*** King sits, he's a few drinks in. He stares at the an early edition of the next day's paper. He takes care to look at every word, every story, headline and page layout. He studies it like a religious man would a holy book. He is methodical and caring.)*

JACOB. How do you know?

JAY. We're all former Reston reporting fellows here, are we not? I'm a natural reporter. It's in my eyes. Jacob Sherman, son of Martin and Gloria Sherman of Ocean Parkway. Father was a CPA, mother taught eighth grade at P.S. 130... As a boy, your mother used to bring you to work sometimes, and the memory of the sweet young girls in your mother's class and the darkness between their thighs still keeps you up at night.

JACOB. I told you that in confidence, J. Edgar.

MONICA. Don't worry Jacob, I'm sure those girls are thinking of you too.

JAY. Look me in the eyes cub reporter Monica Soria, of Lackland Terrace, just inside the 410 on the west side of San Antonio...

MONICA. You are good.

JAY. Your dad, Manny, was a mechanic, and your mother Lucia raised the kids, but made extra money cleaning houses in the Alamo Heights neighborhood, lovingly referred to as "Alamo Whites." You lost your virginity in the eleventh grade to Tyler...

MONICA. Don't you dare.

JACOB. Tyler? Tyler who? Come on.

MONICA. What about you, Jay? Who are you?

(**JAY** *just smiles.*)

JAY. Nothing to say. Okay, here is a secret...a real secret... I'm in love.

MONICA. Oh, that's good. With whom?

JAY. Well, everyday I walk across the Brooklyn Bridge to get to the Police bureau, and every day I stop...*and* I am suspended over the East River looking out at the city, and the port and the clouds and the... It's amazing... I'm in love with the city.

MONICA. Boo.

JACOB. Look at Jay...he's Nick Carraway in Gatsby, on fire for the city. Wide eyed and lovely. I'm envious of that feeling. I grew up here, born with bagel in hand, I'll never have that awe of coming to New York.

MONICA. To New York and all its first impressions.

(*They toast.*)

I want Times gossip. Who is the next executive editor?

JACOB. Bill. He has it all, he comes from the Foreign Desk, he has the requisite Pulitzer, he's been managing editor...tall, very good looking...

JAY. No. I tell you guys...Hal is the pick...he is going to arrive on his white stead and clean that place up...

JACOB. I say, I say...Foghorn Leghorn? That makes about as much sense as Little Bush Junior, who is going to be the next president.

(**FRANK** *notices something, running it over in his head.*)

MONICA. Right on time. Two drinks and the liberal paranoia begins...

JACOB. President George W. Bush, get use to it...it's gonna happen. I'm going to let you in on a little secret, Jay...

FRANK. Do you guys work at the New York Times?

JACOB. ...Americans are fucking idiots.

FRANK. Yeah you do. Who's got a phone? A phone. A mobile… I need to use someone's phone. Can I…?

(**JAY** *fishes for and the retrieves his cell, handing it to* **FRANK**, *who looks at the phone, trying to operate it.*)

How does this…? How the fuck does this fucking thing work?

(**JAY** *takes the phone, manipulating the device.*)

Call the News Desk. Extension 1726…

(**JAY** *does, handing the phone over.* **FRANK** *flops down next to the young writers.*)

(into phone)

Bob? Can I speak to Bob? Bob, it's Frank. Look, there's a typo in the marijuana story on A12. Apple twelve. The pot story. Third graph, half way down. You see it. The sentence with the local "officials officials." Yeah. Also check the age on the Kramer Obit, I saw the AP has him at 87. I don't know…yeah. Fucking amateur hour over there. Would you hang that up for me? Thanks.

JAY. It's ten till one. Isn't the paper closed?

FRANK. They slowed down the presses for updates on California wildfires.

MONICA. Will that fix make any papers?

FRANK. A few. Three dots. Hopefully the one on the publisher's door. You want a drink?

(**MONICA** *and* **JACOB** *decline.*)

Sarah, I'll have another Bombay Dry, up with olives, and…

JAY. Glenlivet neat.

FRANK. A Glenlivet neat? A scotch man. That shit'll kill you. You're a clerk?

JAY. No. Writer. Intermediate. Jay Bennett. Metro.

FRANK. Bennett? Oh. I've seen your byline. You wrote the story about the carpenter getting crushed over here.

JAY. Yeah. It's sad.

FRANK. It's news. Frank King, nice to meet you.

MONICA. Monica Soria…

FRANK. City section, some metro, right?

JACOB. Jacob Sherman.

FRANK. Business desk. Mr. World Wide Web… I know your work. You kids are in the paper a lot. They really let you write now. Used to take years to get a byline…now they hand them out like candy.

JAY. Are you a reporter?

FRANK. Writing is for young men. I'm an editor, I guess…

JAY. What desk do you work at?

FRANK. Me? All of them. None of them. I float around. I've been put out to pasture. I catch typos now. I started as a copy boy forty-three years ago, in March. It's the only job I've ever had. It used to be the grey lady, now the only thing grey is me.

JAY. I never want to work anywhere else.

FRANK. A Timesman, huh? A lifer, because that's what it is…it's a life. Sarah where is that scotch for the thirsty lifer here? They don't drink in the newsroom like they used to… I mean they still put it away, but when I was coming up…oh, man, bottles on the desk, not hidden in a drawer, mind you. Used to be this girl that'd come through and sell sandwiches and beer for lunch… right into the eighties. More likely to find jogging shoes than a bottle of booze nowadays.

JAY. I like those old ways. Hounding. Getting the story. Work hard, play hard. Real…journalism. I wish I could have been born then.

FRANK. You probably don't, really. It wasn't all Woodward and Bernstein. It was… *(beat)* Paul Delaney was the first African American person I ever saw in the newsroom for a long time…not a lot of women either, not because of any… Brilliant men all over…it was just…it was just different…different times. I should go. Sarah, put those on my tab.

(**FRANK** *takes one last look at the paper.*)

Well, guys, I don't know what to tell you. It's a great place to work. Hard to believe that one day…probably… they won't even publish this thing…something that I devoted my entire adult life to will be…gone. They'll tear it down and build a bowling alley.

JAY. There will always be the Times.

FRANK. You think so?

MONICA. Yes. I mean maybe not like this…but the important stuff…the news…I'm sorry, maybe I'm a little drunk…but the heart, the truth…will be disseminated somehow. Electronically, whatever comes next.

FRANK. Oh, to be young. To have so much…idunnowhat. I'm just feeling nostalgic. *(beat)* When I first started working there…my first job was to go down at night and get the papers off the presses, that was when they were still down on the ground floor, and it.. was..amazing. These huge machines…these steel giants, moving so fast. Watching those presses run… watching the papers fly out of them…and I thought, I thought…this is it. This is the pinnacle. This is the future. I'd take the papers up to the editors, and they were still warm…like a newborn baby…and the way the newsprint got on your fingers like…blood… It was a holy thing. Truth and blood. It'll break my heart when it…

JAY. It won't. It's safe.

FRANK. Yeah? Well, that's good. I gotta catch my train or my wife will kill me. One too many Manhattan sleep-overs for me over the years.

JAY. I'll see you around, Frank. Any advice?

FRANK. Change is coming. All you can do is hope the next group of editors, the new masthead, takes a liking to you. Be careful, this place will eat you up if you let it. It'll smash you flat…like that construction worker from your story. Have two for me.

*(***FRANK** *exits.)*

JAY. Sarah, one more! I'm in love.

4

(The hall of Pulitzer Prizes. Eleventh floor of the Times. *Plaques commemorating all the Pulitzer Prizes in Journalism awarded to the paper over the years.)*

(A moment passes and **JUNIOR** *and* **HAL** *Martin enter.)*

*(***HAL** *Martin, 50s, southern gentleman as always, replete in a light suit and his signature panama hat.)*

(The two men take in the years of awards, a leisurely stroll.)

JUNIOR. It's funny, I used to be frightened of the Pulitzer Prize hallway when I was child. It was... The faces of all these old men staring down on me.

HAL. Old men? That's me right there. Ghosts everywhere you look.

JUNIOR. You'd think I'd be used to it. I walk by a bust of my great grandfather - looking through me - in the lobby every morning.

HAL. Must be a hell of a feeling.

JUNIOR. I've been Publisher for almost three years, before that I was preparing for this job...my entire life, working, learning almost every position from the bottom up. And yet, I still feel...

HAL. There is nothing as heavy in this world as the weight of a birthright, Junior.

JUNIOR. You always make me feel so inarticulate, Hal. But, then again, I was never much of a writer, was I?

HAL. Honestly? No, you were never much of a writer, Junior, and that is being kind.

(The men laugh at this.)

But it doesn't matter, you're meant to be the Publisher. That's your calling. I look at you now, and I see a man in bloom.

JUNIOR. You've been head of editorial for how long?

HAL. Seven years. Seven years of opinions.

JUNIOR. Can I ask for one more? *(beat)* An opinion?

HAL. I don't know that you'd want it, but shoot.

JUNIOR. Joe isn't going to be editor indefinitely. When the time comes, it'll be my first important hire.

HAL. Bill will be fine, when the time comes. If that is what you're asking?

JUNIOR. No. Not specifically. I mean. *(beat)* Is that what they're saying? That it's a forgone conclusion... Bill, I mean?

HAL. A blind man could see he's been groomed, Junior. He'll be just fine. He is a man of a moment, perfectly present tense. Besides, isn't he your...? What does your father think?

JUNIOR. I don't know what he thinks, he's no longer Publisher.

HAL. A man in bloom. *(beat)* You know what I see when I look at these walls?

JUNIOR. What?

HAL. A museum. Annals forged by others. History...already written. What I don't see is the future. Do you see it?

JUNIOR. I think so.

HAL. I think you do. You'll do the right thing, Junior. I know it.

(They continue their stroll.)

5

(The Metro desk on deadline. Phones ring while editors shout over cubicles. Controlled chaos.)

*(**BEN** hunches over his keyboard, the computer's monochrome screen illuminates him. Nearby, **JAY**, hovers with a notebook in hand. He dictates to **BEN**.)*

*(**BEN**, having taken the reigns on the story, has **JAY**'s article up. Perhaps it is illuminated above... cursor blinking endlessly.)*

BEN. Your nut graph is too low, you're burying it.

JAY. Nut graph?

BEN. Yes. The graph that tells the reader why it is important to read the story and how the story fits in history. I'm moving it up. Also, this anecdotal lede has to go, it reads like the fucking Wall Street Journal.

JAY. Okay, but...

BEN. *(reading)* "The Rev. Al Sharpton yesterday denounced Mayor Rudolph W. Giuliani's *unyielding* crackdown on homeless people and called *strenuously* on New Yorkers to monitor and report police efforts to sweep the homeless off the streets." Jay, what is with all the verbiage? Christ almighty...

JAY. I'm sorry?

BEN. Is the crackdown really "unyielding?" Is it unable to bend? Is that what you're saying?

JAY. No. I...

BEN. No. *(beat)* And did Sharpton actually call "strenuously?" Did it take *great energy to do it?* Or did he *just call* for this protest?

JAY. He was very...

BEN. The man protests every time Rickey Henderson gets thrown out at home plate... Is he more strenuous than every other time? Come on.

JAY. Well, wait...

BEN. It is inaccurate writing, Jay. This is the Times, we use unassailable language, always. Just say what happened, simply and accurately, please. Report, don't write. *(beat)* We are writing the first draft of history, respect that. Do you understand?

*(A unseen **CLERK** shouts to the duo.)*

CLERK. *(off stage)* News Desk on one! Ben, News Desk on one.

*(**BEN** picks up the phone and then hangs it up without ever bringing it to his ear.)*

BEN. Okay. Okay, are we good to go?

CLERK. *(off stage)* News Desk on one! It's Bob.

*(**BEN** again picks up the phone and hangs it up.)*

BEN. Okay, can I set this?

JAY. No. I have a great quote for the kicker.

*(**FRANK** appears.)*

FRANK. Bob needs the Sharpton story. It is holding up page one.

BEN. It's coming.

FRANK. Seventy-five grand a minute after deadline, Ben. You wanna pay the union overtime?

BEN. What did I just say, Frank?

CLERK. *(off stage)* News Desk on one.

FRANK. Ben, he's threatening to kill the story and run a house ad.

BEN. Bullshit! Jay just got back from this press conference, we have fresh news. We are WORKING HERE!

*(**FRANK** retreating.)*

FRANK. Not my money.

BEN. I need that kicker, Jay!

JAY. *(slowly)* "In the spirit of Martin Luther King," he said, "we'll park our tents in City Hall Park and tell Mayor

Giuliani that we do not want to live in a city that locks up our homeless, but one that lifts up our homeless."

(BEN types furiously.)

BEN. Great. Great. Great kicker.

(BEN finishes his key strokes with authority.)

(Suddenly, there is break in the action. BEN takes a deep breath. Calm after the storm.)

CLERK. *(off stage)* News Desk on one!

(BEN ignores this, looks at JAY.)

BEN. Have you ever seen a man waste seventy-five thousand dollars, Jay?

JAY. No.

CLERK. *(off stage)* Line one, News Desk. They want the Sharpton story! News Desk on one!

(BEN looks at his watch for a full minute, or thereabouts. FRANK returns, lingering around BEN's desk, something is communicated. Tension grows with each passing second, then...)

BEN. Now you have.

(BEN hits a key on the keyboard.)

You have the Sharpton story! Set it and forget it. Goodnight.

(to FRANK)

Thanks, Frank.

(to JAY)

Congrats on page one.

(BEN exits. JAY slumps in the now- vacated seat.)

(A moment passes and JACOB arrives.)

JACOB. That was intense.

JAY. You saw that?

JACOB. The whole newsroom saw it. Guerilla theater at its best.

JAY. It's amazing.

JACOB. Is it always like this over here? Business closes early.

JAY. Working on deadline is like great…sex…or

JACOB. I was going to say we should get a drink, but maybe you need a cigarette.

JAY. The rush…it's a high.

JACOB. We build sandcastles, and we do it again tomorrow.

(JACOB *clumsily drops work from under his arm.*)

JAY. What's with all the photos?

JACOB. Merlin, the photo archive. I couldn't remember some details about the office of this start-up I'm writing about…so I looked at the pictures the photographer filed. Clerk prints them for me.

JAY. There is no such thing as time and space anymore. It's 1986 over here…they still think I use a typewriter. Honestly, I filed a story from my laptop at the scene of a shooting yesterday, I thought they were going burn me for practicing witchcraft.

JACOB. I don't know how you work on deadline like that. Can I ask you something? Aren't you ever scared of your cursor?

JAY. The cursor?

JACOB. Sometimes I sit here and I just stare…and…I'm terrified. It goes away, but there is a moment, almost every day, where I think… "I can't write. I can't do it." Does that happen to you?

JAY. No. Don't write, report. Make another phone call.

JACOB. I hate you. *(beat)* I have this recurring dream… where I'm on deadline…for what? I don't know, but its big and I'm behind…and the phone keeps ringing and ringing but I don't pick it up, I can't even look at it. Finally it stops, but I'm soaked in sweat, in a complete panic...and I start to cough. I cough hard until my teeth fall out in my hands and then...out of my mouth comes a ringing cell phone. Then I wake up.

JAY. First round is on me. I'm on page one.

(They exit.)

6

(The smoking room. A dingy former office, now allocated for the dwindling number of smokers left at the paper. A few chairs, tables with ashtrays heaped full of butts. There is a window that looks out onto nothing and barely allows the distant neon light from Times Square in.)

*(**GERALD** Haynes sits and smokes in silence, lost in thought. A moment passes, and **JAY** enters.)*

*(The two men nod to one another, a simple gesture between strangers, an office hello. **JAY** lights a cigarette and picks up a section of the paper that is nearby, he glances at it halfheartedly. **JAY**, pulls deep on his smoke...)*

JAY. Gerald?

GERALD. Hm?

JAY. I'm Jay Bennett. I...

GERALD. Yeah.

JAY. I'm a reporter with Metro. We met during my first orientation. Then again at a meeting of the minority hires, you gave a speech and...

GERALD. I remember, Jay. Hello.

(They each pull on their cigarettes.)

Sorry, I'm just...work on my mind.

JAY. I understand.

GERALD. Sorry. I've been in management for eight years and I still don't completely understand...nevermind. So, how's Metro treating you?

JAY. Good. Great, I mean. I'm working at the police bureau. I'm in the paper a lot.

GERALD. I know.

JAY. I guess you would. The only bad thing is...I started smoking. Just part of the lifestyle, I guess.

GERALD. What do they say? Starting is easy. Quitting is hard. I started when the Post-Dispatch sent me to Washington the first time. That was '77 or so… I've been quitting ever since.

JAY. Stress reliever. Digit to oral… I dunno. A lot of reporters smoke.

GERALD. Back then, when I started, everybody smoked. Didn't trust you otherwise… It was the only way you could get a source alone was to take a smoke break. Just the way it was.

JAY. Washington. That's… I mean.

GERALD. Washington is hazardous to your health. They should post that on the sign leading into town.

JAY. Great for your career though.

GERALD. Always news there, that's for sure.

JAY. I want to work in Washington. New York, Washington then Foreign.

GERALD. That's all? You lack ambition, son.

JAY. "A man's worth is no greater than the worth of his ambitions," Marcus Aurellius.

GERALD. "Ambition is the last refuge of failure," Oscar Wilde. There is a quote for fucking everything. *(Beat)* D.C., huh?

JAY. It's my home town, so… Yeah. My father works for the military… Pentagon. Army brat. We traveled a lot, but D.C. is home. You?

GERALD. St. Louis. MIZ-ZOU.

JAY. Missouri J-school..Great school.

GERALD. Could be. Sometimes. 1960's Missouri, man…

JAY. I imagine.

GERALD. You should have seen me, called myself Uganda X – big ol' afro. Where did we find you, Jay?

JAY. University of Maryland.

GERALD. Terrapins. Wupped the Tigers' ass this year in basketball. You and me might be the only non-Ivys around here, but at least we have basketball teams to root for. Saddest thing in the world is an Ivy League basketball game.

JAY. "A thrilling game Cornell edges Harvard, ten to eight."

(They laugh.)

Can I have a cigarette?

GERALD. Menthol, alright?

JAY. Thank you.

GERALD. You hear the joke about Kwanzaa Claus? You know, the black Santa Claus?

JAY. No.

GERALD. What do you leave out instead of milk and cookies for Kwanzaa Claus?

JAY. What?

GERALD. Pack of menthols and Kool-aid.

(They laugh.)

I love a good racist joke, they make me laugh.

JAY. Where did you hear that?

GERALD. Right here.

JAY. At the Times? Somebody told that to you?

GERALD. No. I was in the elevator. They didn't see me there…which is a feat in and of itself. So, these two guys who shall remain nameless, pop off with that joke…and I started laughing harder than either of them. You should have seen the look on their faces. Oh, boy, that was a fun eight floors up.

JAY. Amazing.

GERALD. That sorta stuff doesn't bother me. It's the little things. When I was Metro editor before getting this AME job, they used to slug all the murder stories involving young black men…so a lot of stories…they used to slug them all "Black." So every day I'd come in, turn on my computer and look on the Atex system and see days worth of homicide stories piled up, date then slug...01back, 02black, 03black one after another...they didn't know any better. A room full of brilliant, overeducated, bleeding-heart and generally well intentioned people...they just didn't see how that could make a black person feel. *(beat)* Anyway, I got them to start slugging those stories "Slay."

JAY. Gerald, I just want to say, you are a real inspiration to us all...and all the things they say...

GERALD. What do they say?

JAY. I mean, just being the Jackie Robinson of the Times and all...

GERALD. Jackie Robinson, huh?

JAY. It just means a lot to the black employees...

GERALD. I'm not Jackie Robinson or Mother Teresa or anybody else... I'm just an Assistant Managing Editor who happens to be black, and you, my boy, are just a writer. Sure, time was, at this place they stuck the niggers in sports, the queens in culture and women could cover spring fashion, if they were lucky - everything else was covered by the landed gentry. Time was...but from the top on down, we're trying to make this newsroom reflect the diversity of the city. It's hard and may not happen fast...

JAY. Why not? Kick that door down.

GERALD. You want it all and you want it now...you remind me of... Maybe we should call you Uganda X?

*(**GERALD** stamps out his cigarette.)*

You're a talented writer, Jay. I assume you know the difference between on the record and off the record, right?

JAY. Yes, sir.

GERALD. Well this is all off...you work twice as hard as all the others, and you never open your mouth no matter what you hear, you just smile.

*(**GERALD** smiles.)*

You smile and do good work, and then and move up the ladder…where you can make a difference. Then you get home, pour a drink for you and your wife and you yell like a motherfucker about all these sonsabitches. *(Beat)* Keepworking hard, because people are watching you.

(GERALD *gives* **JAY** *another cigarette and exits.)*

7

(A phone call between two offices. One, the Times *newsroom, the second is the Police Bureau. On one phone is* **BEN**, *on the other,* **JAY**. *Both sit in front of their computers.* **JAY** *lets the phone ring before answering it.)*

JAY. *(answering)* Cop Shop. Bennett.

BEN. Jay. It's Ben.

JAY. Hey Ben, can I call you back?

BEN. Did you get my email?

JAY. Yeah. No. I mean, what?

BEN. I sent you an email about a correction.

JAY. Correction?

BEN. Yes, Jay, I sent it this morning. It's now two o'clock.

JAY. I didn't see it, Ben. I'm not in front of my computer.

BEN. Jay…

JAY. I'll check and get back to you. I do have to call you back…

BEN. Jay.

JAY. Yes, Ben.

BEN. I called your land line, not your cell. Now, can you please just look at the correction in your email? This is becoming tiresome, Jay.

JAY. I know…I know you called the land line, I just…I picked up my line at the clerk's desk.

BEN. Fine. Put me on hold, go to your desk…bring up the email so we can do this.

*(***JAY*** puts ***BEN*** on hold.* ***JAY*** *takes a moment then checks his email.* ***JAY*** *then picks up the phone again.)*

JAY. What is the email called?

BEN. The subject is "CX," meaning correction. Just like the previous three times, Jay. It's from your Monday shooting story.

JAY. I don't…oh, here it is. Oh, yeah. So.

BEN. The correction is saying the perp is from the Bronx, not Jersey as you reported, and the victim, we are identifying as the son of the owner of the store, not the owner. This is pretty basic stuff here, Jay.

JAY. I'm checking my notes. Can you just hold on a sec...

(*JAY puts BEN on hold. He takes a minute, flipping through a reporters' pad. JAY takes BEN off of hold.*)

I...ah...yeah. Yeah. This is my bad. I mixed up some old notes here, I guess. First reports were that the victim was the owner of the jewelry shop...then later the father, who actually own the shop, found the body...so, yeah...the kid just worked there.

BEN. Does the correction read all right? I mean, are we straight now?

JAY. Yeah. We are...I'm sorry. I just.

BEN. You know the Times doesn't have fact checkers, right? Aside from the copy and backfield desks, it's an honor system for the reporters.

JAY. I know.

BEN. Your work has been slipping, Jay. It isn't acceptable. Now I know you have had some editing corrections, but this is too much... This is a reoccurring problem...

JAY. I know. I've been diligent about my notes.

BEN. You've been exceedingly sloppy. I want to have a sit down with you and Nancy, it's just not acceptable.

JAY. I know. It won't happen again.

BEN. If you have a problem, if there is something going on that I need to know about, let me know.

JAY. I've just been working really hard. Really.

BEN. I understand that. We're all working *really* hard, Jay. Okay? We all are. Is Nancy still your 8i supervisor?

JAY. Yes.

BEN. I'm gonna email Nancy and set something up.

JAY. Okay. If you feel like this is necessary.

BEN. Shape up, Jay, or you're not going to be at the Times much longer.

*(***BEN*** hangs up.* **JAY***, receiver in hand, crumbles.)*

8

*(A restaurant dinner table. **HAL** and **GERALD**, martinis half gone, a dinner before them.)*

GERALD. Since '83, when I came over from Post-Dispatch for the election.

HAL. That's right. You had to follow H.W. Bush for how long? You poor sonofabitch. Well, it could have been worse, you could have been assigned Walter Mondale, he might have bored you straight to death, then you wouldn't be here today.

(They laugh.)

Feels a lot longer, like a lifetime ago, but also…no time at all.

GERALD. Strange how that happens. Sentiment aside…may I ask?

HAL. I'm sorry?

GERALD. We've known each other long enough to be forthright with one another. *(beat)* I like our meals, Hal, but there is usually a reason for them.

HAL. There's the man I'm looking for. Direct. To the point. I've been talking to Junior…

GERALD. I know. Everybody knows, Hal.

HAL. I'm on the one yard line for the big job, Gerald, and I wanted to talk to you.

GERALD. Executive Editor. Congratulations. What do you want to talk to me about?

HAL. We always shared something, you and I, an understanding, haven't we?

GERALD. I've always thought so.

HAL. I'm going to get this job over Bill because I have sold Junior on my vision of the future of this newspaper. I'm going to need people, strong people like you, to help me implement it.

GERALD. Strong people.

HAL. I told Junior, and I firmly believe it, that the paper has gotten old and soft. That it must adapt or die. It's evolution. Pure and simple. From the top down, I'm going to change the way this paper operates. I want to kick start the paper's competitive metabolism. Reinvigorate the staff, get young hungry reporters eating and breathing their jobs again…fighting for stories, breaking news. We need to get people reading the paper with interest again – not because they feel like they have to. For years, we have been the journalistic spinach jammed down the throat of America; sure, it's good for you but it tastes like shit. It's time to change…we have to be mouth watering and delectable. This newspaper has to be irresistible. I care too much to watch it crumble to dust because it was too damn stodgy and old fashioned to change. We need better writing, better editing… I want the stories to sing and have sweep. I want better storytelling.

GERALD. And good reporting…

HAL. Of course, good reporting. But, is it too damn much to ask for a news story to read better than the back of a tube of tooth paste? I think not. They called it The Grey Lady, not because of the grey photos, but because of the grey writing. Dull and lifeless. *(beat)* We are on the precipice, my friend, it is do or die time… and I think you know it.

GERALD. Where do I fit in?

HAL. Right at the top.

GERALD. Are you offering me the managing editorship?

HAL. You know how much I respect you, Gerald. We have history. In any revolution, you need generals and soldiers. Can I count on you?

(**GERALD** *smiles.*)

9

(The last vestiges of a small Christmas party (2000). The three young reporters sit around a coffee table in JAY's apartment.)

MONICA. Oh, this again…it's bullshit, Jay…bullshit…

JACOB. Now that you started, I gotta hear it.

JAY. It's from a friend of a friend of a friend…

JACOB. So you're sourced…

JAY. According to her, Mark Greenberg, the city comptroller…

MONICA. The *married* city comptroller and democratic candidate for mayor of New York City, mind you…

JACOB. Five bucks to anybody who can tell me what a comptroller does…

JAY. Anyway, apparently the comptroller is sleeping with his secretary. And Mark likes to fuck at the office after hours, and according to this friend of mine, when they are doing it and he reaches his crescendo…

MONICA. The point of no return.

JAY. Right before he comes…he screams, "You know who you're fucking? The first Jewish President of the United States!"

MONICA. That's my favorite part. He doesn't just blurt it out once in a fit of passion…he screams it every time, it's like his catch phrase.

JAY. I think I'm going to write about it.

JACOB. What? Maybe if we worked for the Weekly World News.

JAY. Oh yeah, sex scandals involving politicians are *never* news. Just ask Bill Clinton.

JACOB. You are not serious? Because it's a rumor.

JAY. It's got great details, though.

JACOB. It's fun, but it's a rumor. *(beat)* But, then again, what do I know? Everything is backwards... Up is down, down is up. Hell, we just had a man who is seemingly handicapped steal the presidential election... I know nothing.

JAY. I know... I'm joking.

JACOB. Believe me...one day...one day, I'll cast away my allegiance to the truth and quit...write my novel and become wildly successful...then..

MONICA. Here we go...

JACOB. ...and then become an eccentric recluse out in Maine or someplace. Maybe teach a little...

MONICA. What's the novel going to be called?

JACOB. What do you think it should it be called?

MONICA. "Daddy Issues," what else? I'll believe it when I see it.

JACOB. I'm sorry, is this *so unbelievable?*

MONICA. Do you know how many unfinished novels are stashed in bottom drawers in the newsroom? Laid one on top of the other, they'd stretch from here to the moon. *(laughing)* I think it is hilarious.

JACOB. Why?

MONICA. It is *the* definition of white people problems... am I a journalist or a novelist? That a person would struggle with what "sort" of writer they are going to be... I find it hilarious. Where I grew up, the idea of being *any* type of writer is completely absurd. My mother tells my friends back home that I'm a trapeze artist, because it's more believable than me writing for a newspaper, much less one in New York City.

JACOB. And yet, my parents are still disappointed I'm not a lawyer.

MONICA. Pobrecito.

JAY. *(far away)* I've never wanted to write a novel or be a lawyer... This is what I always wanted to do. Write for the paper.

MONICA. Jay? Are you alright?

(**JAY** *chokes back something inside, he exits the room.* **MONICA** *and* **JACOB**, *alone now, discreetly kiss. A moment passes, and* **JAY** *returns.*)

JAY. I'm sorry. After my father died, I remember reading his obituary in the paper, it was…after that… You know what I asked for that year for my birthday? The Best Newspaper Writing, 1990-91…and every year since.

(**JAY** *reveals the well-worn book, then slams it on the coffee table.* **JAY** *slumps.*)

MONICA. What's a matter honey?

JAY. They're not going to hire me.

MONICA. What are you talking about? You're in the paper all the time, doing great work.

JACOB. Did they say they weren't going to hire you?

JAY. I've…I've had a lot of corrections lately.

MONICA. Every writer has corrections.

JAY. I've had more than…I just, Monica…it's not good. I've just been writing so many fucking stories…and I'm not even important, just filling pages with shorts about shootings and rapes. Feeding the machine. CXrape, CXshoot, CX…CX…CX…the corrections. I had to have a meeting with Ben and Nancy a couple of days ago. They gave me a warning. I felt like Ben wanted to get rid of me right there.

JACOB. I thought he liked you?

JAY. Not anymore. I feel like he looks at me and… Then Nancy pointed out that my corrections fall in an acceptable statistical area. You should have seen the look on Ben's face…he wants me gone. He hates me.

MONICA. He doesn't hate you. It's going to be okay.

JAY. No, it's not. It's the fucking Times! It's my life.

JACOB. You're a good writer. You are going to be a great writer. You just need to bone up a little bit. You've got time to change minds.

JAY. I'm sorry. I'm so sorry. You're right. You're both right... I'm just... I'm just fucked up, I guess. Hell of a host, huh?

(*JAY retrieves a glassine bag of coke from his pocket and pours a pile on the coffee table.*)

MONICA. Jay, I think...

JAY. Come on. Let's get this party going...we can gossip or something. Monica, there's more vodka.

MONICA. I've had enough to drink.

JAY. Jacob, you aren't leaving till this is gone.

JACOB. Last time I did coke, I ended up trying to explain the entire plot of *The Lord of the Rings* to a girl on the L train. I'll pass.

JAY. Come on.

JACOB. It goes back in the bag, Jay...you know that, right?

JAY. I can't have this shit in the house.

MONICA. Jay, I'm sorry but, I gotta get back to Manhattan.

JACOB. Yeah. Where are you? West Village, right? Wanna share a cab?

JAY. Wait, wait, wait. You can't leave.

JACOB. It's been a long night, it's already two...

JAY. You can't leave me here alone. I'm high and a little sad. it's...come on, guys. I JUST POURED MY FUCKING HEART OUT TO YOU!

(*JAY laughs. An awkward silence.*)

I'm sorry. I'm so sorry.

JACOB. Jay, it's just, I have reporting to do tomorrow. So do you. I should have gone to bed hours ago.

JAY. I'm sorry. I'm an idiot. Wait, I have more good gossip. Have you heard about al-Gaddafi and the Times' own Ms. Miller...they had an affair, and he had her wrapped in a giant Persian rug and delivered to him... SO, they unfurl the rug and out pours a scantily clad Ms. Harris...

JACOB. Save some for the office…and if you can't sleep just read your "Best Newspaper Writing, 1990-91," that'll put you right down.

(**JAY**, *despite himself, smiles.*)

MONICA. We can catch something on 7th Avenue, right?

JAY. You two. Who are you kidding?

MONICA. What?

JAY. I am a good reporter. I notice things. I know what's going on with you two… It's obvious.

JACOB. *(smiling)* What? Jay…

MONICA. You can't tell anybody.

JAY. You're my friends. You didn't think you could tell me?

MONICA. We just wanted to keep it on the down low. It wasn't personal.

JACOB. Office relationships. They're… You understand? Besides, it's never going to work out. She's Mexican, I'm Jewish… I'm afraid our kids will end up being too lazy to control the economy.

JAY. I won't say anything. I'm happy for you both. Stay. Let's celebrate.

MONICA. The night has got to end sometime.

JAY. Does it? I'm not joking. Are you guys mad at me? I'm sorry about earlier… I didn't mean to ruin the party.

JACOB. Let's do this, if we're going to do this. Jay, it's gonna be alright, man… I know it. Hasta Manana.

(**MONICA** *kisses* **JAY** *on the forehead, like a mother would a child.*)

MONICA. Go to bed, Jay.

JACOB. Merry Christmas.

(*They all say goodbye, both colleagues exit.* **JAY** *sits alone. He does a line of coke.* **JAY** *picks up his phone and dials. A short moment passes.*)

JAY. *(into phone)* Mom? Mom, it's Jay. Everything is okay. I'm fine. I know it's early, but… I just wanted to hear your voice. I know. I'm sorry. I just was thinking. I. I miss dad. I just… I don't know what I was thinking. I'm sorry I woke you up. I'll call you later. This is all a dream..a dream.

(**JAY** *hangs up.*)

10

(The Newsroom staff has gathered for an announcement. **JUNIOR**, *the publisher, stands on a landing, beside him are* **HAL** *and* **GERALD**.*)*

JUNIOR. It's in vogue these days to declare the death of the newspaper at the hands of the internet, just as we were declared dead when the radio arrived, and again when television news became popular. I say this not to minimize this threat, but to declare that we must embrace this challenge and I can think of no better person, no better leader, than Hal Martin. Before bringing his fearless voice to the Editorial page, Hal was a distinguished writer for the paper, having reported from the Mississippi delta to the Beltway to the House of Lords, culminating in a Pulitzer Prize in feature writing for his personal essay, "Lessons from Nel," depicting his childhood friendship with his family's African American housekeeper and the lasting gift of their relationship. As an editor, Hal has proved to have an amazing news sense and more importantly, has proved to be a great leader of men and women. It is this last quality that most attracted me to Hal when considering all the qualified candidates for this job… that and the fact he promised to teach me to fly fish. In all seriousness, we're entering a new and exciting age in the newspaper business, and that calls for a new and exciting Executive Editor. Hal, would you like to address your newsroom?

HAL. Certainly. First off, I want to thank you, Junior, for this opportunity. As for my predecessor, Joe… I can only hope when I take over I'll be able to maintain the level of excellence that you have set as our standard.

*(***HAL*** applauds.)*

I do want to confirm the worst kept secret in journalism and announce my choice as Managing Editor, Gerald Haynes. Gerald is a trusted colleague and more importantly, a friend whose news judgment is unquestioned. He was a recent recipient of the NABJ Journalist of the Year Award for heading up and editing our ground-breaking series on race, a great honor. I can tell you, Gerald and I share the many of the same beliefs and passions…but differ enough that I know he'll tell me to shut up when I need to be told to shut up.

(Laughter. **HAL** *applauds* **GERALD***, who stands uncomfortably.)*

I have spent my entire adult life newpapering, including the last twenty-three years here at the Times…and I can honestly say that I love this newspaper. But we cannot be complacent. One of my first editors used to say, "If you are going to be a bear, be a grizzly." But, I'm from Alabama, so if I'm going to be a bear, I'm gonna be Bear Bryant…and Coach Bryant used to say "I'm no miracle man. I guarantee nothing but hard work." And we will work hard… We are going to push to find the biggest stories of our times, and cover them comprehensively and with flare. We are not going to wait for news to happen and react, we are going to seek the news…and then we are going to flood the zone with our brightest and most talented journalists. Coach Bryant had another saying…"Get winners into the game," and Gerald and I are going to. With challenge comes opportunity, so I challenge you…where are my winners?

(JUNIOR, **HAL** *and* **GERALD** *pose for a photo together. It is projected above, then fades.)*

11

(BEN in his office. GERALD enters.)

GERALD. Ben, do you have a minute?

BEN. Gerald, what brings you down from on high?

GERALD. I was CC'd on an email about the new hires. I want to talk to you about Jay Bennett.

BEN. What about him?

GERALD. Why do you oppose his hiring?

BEN. I'm his editor. I offered my opinion. I don't think he's up to the Times standards.

GERALD. Explain yourself.

BEN. I thought I just did. He has a lot of corrections. He has bad work habits. He is…flighty.

GERALD. How so?

BEN. He is hard to get a hold of… He takes the company car and I never know where he is.

GERALD. He has published three hundred and eleven stories for this paper. Three hundred and eleven. How is it he can put that many stories in the paper, most of them in your section, and yet, still not be qualified to work here? Shit, I know staffers…guys that have been here for twenty years that don't put that many stories in the paper over five years. Staffers.

BEN. He is prolific, but so is MacDonald's…

GERALD. He's hungry. These new kids work different than what we are use to, what we came up learning. Things change.

BEN. Some things don't. I don't like style over substance.

GERALD. Style? Is style coded language? People use to complain about Arthur Ashe's style…

(Silence. The men examine one another.)

BEN. If Jay were white, would we be having this conversation?

GERALD. Chose your words carefully, Ben.

BEN. We can't drop our standards in the name of diversity, Gerald.

GERALD. Is that what's happening?

BEN. If we hire Jay, then I believe yes.

GERALD. I disagree and I resent the implication.

BEN. Odd, you and I normally see eye to eye on most things.

GERALD. Spare me your sarcasm.

BEN. Jay Bennett shouldn't write for The New York Times.

GERALD. I've been dealing with men like you my entire life.

BEN. Men like me?

GERALD. Yes. You pray at the altar of your own certainty, but at the end of the day, you're nothing more than a run of the mill…

BEN. What? A bigot? You should listen to yourself, Gerald. Whatever personal differences you and I have, I've always put the paper first. Always.

GERALD. Be that as it may, I disagree with your assessment of Jay, as does Hal. His stories sing.

BEN. Sing? This isn't an opera.

GERALD. We think there is a star there…

BEN. Star? You're going to be sitting in the big chair, Gerald. You got the big job.

GERALD. That's right.

BEN. Use it. I have no control over what you can do. But, I can tell you this, I don't want Jayson Bennett working on my desk. Get him out of Metro, I don't care where.

12

(Smith's bar.)

(JAY, possibly high and definitely drunk, has a small celebration alone. MONICA enters, she's upset.)

JAY. Monica...beautiful Monica...

MONICA. Jay. I was looking for you.

JAY. I was looking for another drink. Sarah. Whatever the lovely Ms. Soria wants.

MONICA. Can I talk to you?

JAY. I have an announcement. You're speaking to a full time employee...a staff member...of the The New York Times. They hired me. I'm out of Metro. They're going to detach me, I don't know where yet, but...

MONICA. Oh. That's great, Jay. That's really great...

JAY. You were right. When I doubted...you were right. Thank you.

MONICA. I'm happy for you.

(MONICA, fighting it, begins to weep.)

JAY. What happened?

MONICA. Nothing.

JAY. What's wrong? Jacob? Something wrong with Jacob?

MONICA. They aren't going to hire me.

JAY. Oh, Monica.

MONICA. They let me go. I went to meet with Nancy, I thought it was a just a chat...a check in, to see how I was doing.

JAY. No. Shit. They can't.

MONICA. They did. They just did. They were exceedingly formal, "thank you for your contributions to the paper..." But then I asked why...what didn't I do? Nancy just said, I haven't shown the ability to consistently break news...and that I lacked an authoritative voice. They criticized my voice...

JAY. Your voice. I don't understand.

MONICA. They offered me recommendations if I want…

JAY. I've seen your byline…read all your stories.

MONICA. They said, I could stay and work freelance… I could write Neediest Cases? Clerk… Answer phones? I'm ruining your celebration. I feel sick.

JAY. Sit. It'll be alright.

MONICA. I feel like I've been in a car accident. Everything is… *(beat)* Do I go back to San Antonio? My family… what do I say?

JAY. Where is Jacob?

MONICA. I haven't told him yet. He. I just couldn't. *(beat)* I can't stop thinking. I saw "Our Town" when I was a girl at this little community theater. It was sad and happy, all these different things…and there is this part when the Stage Manager announces that a new bank is under construction…and he believes it would be a good idea to place a time capsule in the cornerstone of the bank…and he says if he had his way, the capsule would contain a copy of the local paper, the U.S. Constitution, the Bible, Shakespeare's works and the Times…The New York Times. He says it would enable people "a thousand years from now to know a few simple facts about us." It was the first I heard of the Times…but I knew it was important. I knew I wanted to be a part of it. To record a few simple facts about our time.

JAY. I'll call Gerald. I just wrote the TimesTalk article about him being appointed Managing Editor. He and I are tight.

MONICA. No. Jay. What are you talking about?

JAY. I'm just saying, we can do something.

(**JAY** *takes* **MONICA** *into his arms, a consoling gesture, the hug lingers.* **JAY** *sloppily tries to kiss* **MONICA**, *who recoils.*)

MONICA. What are you doing? Why would you try…?

JAY. Come on. I wanted to make you feel better.

MONICA. Like that? Who are you?

JAY. I'm me. You understand me...us...no one else does, not Jacob.

MONICA. Jacob?

JAY. What about him? You came to me. Just now.

MONICA. A friend.

JAY. Who did you look for? Me. You thought of me. Not Jacob. That's the answer. Jacob isn't like us.

MONICA. Jacob is your friend and my...

JAY. He's...he'll never...you know...understand. Your mother cleaned the houses of people like him...

MONICA. What are you talking about?

JAY. Let's start over. *(beat)* You were so sad... I wanted to make you feel better. I feel so happy. I thought together... Please.

MONICA. I don't know what to say...

JAY. Say. Say what I want you to say. *(beat)* I need a drink. Sarah? I need a drink.

MONICA. Don't keep drinking, Jay. It won't help anything.

JAY. I just wanted you to feel the way I feel. I was so happy.

MONICA. You can't make it better, Jay. I didn't come to you for you to make it better. I just wanted to talk... I just needed you to listen... I should go.

JAY. You shouldn't be alone.

MONICA. It's okay to be alone sometimes, Jay.

*(**MONICA** goes to leave. Stopping.)*

Congratulations, Jay. Really.

*(**MONICA** exits.)*

13

(New slide: A picture of an airliner in mid-flight, behind it a bright blue sky.)

(Sixth slide: the picture of the airliner, only it is not cropped. The airline is streaming toward the World Trade Center.)

(The deafening sound of a phone ringing.)

ACT II

14

(Slide redux: A picture of an airliner in mid-flight, behind it a bright blue sky.)

(Second slide redux: the picture of the airliner, only it is not cropped. The airline is streaming toward the World Trade Center.)

(The sounds of the newsroom of the Times*...first phones ringing then being slammed, editors shout to reporters,* **CLERK**'s *calling for editors, presses run. The sounds of the 9/11 attacks are added...then images from the anthrax attacks.)*

(Other images are shown. Pictures of the 9/11 aftermath, and pictures of the invasion of Afghanistan and Iraq. Leaders and villains, Bush, Karzai, Hussien, Bin Laden...)

(As the images come at us faster and faster, the noises of the newsroom come to a cacophony. Blackout. Silence.)

*(*New York Times *newsroom, after hours.* **HAL** *Martin, a few drinks in, holds court. Nearby we find* **JUNIOR** *and* **GERALD**.*)*

HAL. Six days. It was the sixth day of my editorship and it was chaos...outside. But only outside. I walked through the lobby, and people were already gathering, some with photos of their loved ones... Thinking we could help. A woman grabbed my shoulder on the way in and asked me to help find her daughter...there was nothing I could say to her. Outside, it was chaos. Inside, in the newsroom, it was this incredible quiet, so quiet it reminded me of a snow fall. That has always amazed me, that when things are the most chaotic... when major news breaks...a newsroom will become silent. Like a champion runners' heart that beats slow when the body is most taxed. By the time I got there, we were already humming, a body at work, a living thing. Professional individuals working in concert... it was beautiful to behold. Employees walking from all over the city, dust in their hair, rushing to the office to work. They just wanted to work. Photographers and writers on the scene, risking everything...to get the story. We knew about what everybody else knew, which is to say, nothing. Spotty phones and misinformation...but we put out a paper. We put out one hell of a paper. And every day after. *(beat)* I believe the papers produced during that period will stand the test of time. More importantly, we honored all those lives by bringing to our readers an accurate, balanced record of the crisis. A record. *(beat)* We all want to be remembered, don't we? Above all else. That's the most human thing - the want to be recorded, recalled - immortal. At the heart of it, we want to outlive death in the memory of those who come after. *(beat)* I'm proud of the work we did. Not because of the these awards we are celebrating tonight, far from. No. I'm proud that when the bell rang, we answered. That we *have always* answered when called to...and always will. A constant. We need to be, otherwise...

(**HAL** *lights a cigar for himself, and the others. He looks at the flame of his match or candle, at the light it gives.*)

This is what we did. This is what we do. Illuminate the darkness...we shed light on the events of this world. A newspaper is a tool, a device, that shows us...what's out there. What we are, who we are...shows us what the world looks like. These awards, if nothing else, are a testament to that...a testament to all of us, but especially you and your family, Junior. Where would the city be without your paper? Without our "Portraits of Grief?" Where would America be without The New York Times?

(**HAL** *raises a glass.*)

Gentleman. To illumination…

15

(Smith's bar)

(JACOB drunkenly rants to an unseen bartender. JAY enters without JACOB noticing.)

JACOB. This arrogant bastard...thinks he can force the entire world to do think his way. He thinks he has a mandate to shape everybody in his image. He is the worst type of ideologue, one who plays on people's fears and insecurities. Do you know what I hate most about him? His certainty. That blind certainty.

JAY. You're a journalist. You are supposed to be impartial... you shouldn't talk about President Bush that way.

JACOB. I'm not talking about Bush, I'm talking about Hal Martin, our boss.

(quoting)

"'Tis the Times' plague when madmen lead the blind." *(beat)* Well. Well. Well.

JAY. Jacob. This place is empty...

JACOB. Everybody is afraid they're going to get blown up. On the plus side, we can get great tickets to *The Producers*.

JAY. But you're here...I was hoping to see a friendly face...

JACOB. Is that what I am? At a bar, no less. I thought you quit.

JAY. I did. Bar *and* restaurant. Sarah, can I get a cheese fries, with gravy, and fried mozzarella sticks...and a soda with cran, please?

JACOB. That's what you're having for dinner? What are you, fifteen? Gives me a stomachache just thinking about it...and no booze?

JAY. Moderation in all things...

JACOB. Including moderation. Long time, no see. Weeks and weeks. What are you doing here? Aren't you supposed to be...somewhere, reporting on something wonderful and exciting?

JAY. Expenses.

JACOB. They have fax machines. E-mail. Snail mail.

JAY. I had a meeting with Jim.

JACOB. Ah. The life of a national writer...whisked from city to city. What is it now? The shooter in DC?

JAY. They knew I was sourced down there...

JACOB. A great story.

JAY. Yeah. The sniper today...I think they're going to detach me, do war stuff, dead soldiers. Then...?

JACOB. Then?

JAY. Iraq maybe?

JACOB. Foreign.

JAY. Foreign. Hunting big game. The war.

JACOB. I can't say I'm not jealous. You lucky motherfucker.

JAY. Lucky?

JACOB. No. Not lucky. I'm drunk. Man, this sniper thing... It's a great story. But I can't complain, you know what else is a great story? Writing about the incremental daily recovery of the city's post attack economy.

(**JAY** *laughs.*)

Hey! Got me on the front page. Otherwise, I'm trying to support all these struggling small businesses one drink at a time.

JAY. You should ask out of Bizday. The whole world is falling to pieces. They're dying for writers on National.

JACOB. They must be, you're working there.

JAY. You asshole. What I'm saying is...the economy is never a story.

JACOB. Sure it is. It's just a boring story.

JAY. There are bigger out there...

JACOB. It's not sexy, but it's big...the fucking economy brought the fall of Rome. What are you doing here? Weren't you in Virginia this morning? I saw that brief on the web...

JAY. They have these new things, planes, you should check them out sometime...

JACOB. Seriously.

JAY. What?

JACOB. What are you doing here, Jay? Aren't they still looking for this guy?

JAY. Yes.

JACOB. Shouldn't you...

JAY. I told you...

JACOB. Expenses? Nothing you couldn't do on the telephone.

JAY. No. It had to be face to face.

JACOB. With Jim?

JAY. I told you. What is this?

JACOB. They only thing Jim wants to talk face to face about is the Grateful Dead.

JAY. You *are* drunk.

JACOB. What are you doing here, Jay?

JAY. I don't like the way you're asking, Jacob.

JACOB. Tell me. Tell me the truth.

JAY. I am.

(Silence, a hard stare. A breath.)

JACOB. It's a girl, isn't it?

JAY. What?

JACOB. You...have a girl up here in the city. Come on. We used to be pretty close...who is it?

JAY. Yep. You got me.

JACOB. I knew it. Who?

JAY. You don't know her...

JACOB. Or do I? Someone at the paper? Come on... I don't get any gossip since you left.

JAY. Just a girl, you don't know her.

JACOB. She coming here?

JAY. Maybe later.

JACOB. That's good, man. That's good. You spent too much time at the paper…you needed a life outside…that's good… Just. Yeah. I'm happy for you.

JAY. It's great. She's great. How's Monica? I only saw her once since the…

JACOB. Monica? She, ah…she left. She's gone.

JAY. Did I just miss her?

JACOB. No. I mean, she left the city. She stuck around for a while, but then the attack…the…there was no work. I told her I loved her and asked her to move in with me, but she decided to go back home.

JAY. Home?

JACOB. Texas. She got a job offer at a paper down there, her dad's sick…so. It just made sense.

JAY. You two?

JACOB. Nope. That's, ah… We email every once in awhile… Fuck.

JAY. She left.

JACOB. After the paper didn't renew her… Every time she saw me, Jay…every time she was reminded about the paper and her dreams and…I could tell she hated me, resented… It was a death sentence, her not getting a job there…but it was a slow, painful death. It's a church, this place…a religion, and…you have to marry within your religion…otherwise…

JAY. I'm sorry.

JACOB. For what?

JAY. For you.

JACOB. It's for the best. I miss her. It's probably… I don't have time for women, anyway. How do you have time?

JAY. I don't know. I work fast, I guess.

JACOB. I think I should go home soon.

JAY. Stay, we can talk.

JACOB. No. I'm drunk. I work tomorrow…and you have a flight, I presume.

JAY. Train. Tonight.

JACOB. Tonight? She must be very good and very…fast.

JAY. She is.

JACOB. I'm very…proud of you, Jay. Really…you are doing a great job. Remember me when you run this paper.

JAY. I'll call you next time I'm in town.

JACOB. Do that. You still live in Park Slope?

JAY. I live in hotels, but I got the room there still.

JACOB. I moved not too far from you. It's funny actually… maybe it's not.

JAY. What?

JACOB. I thought I saw you on the street the other day. I was hoisting a couch at the time…so I didn't call out. But I could've sworn…

JAY. I wasn't here.

JACOB. I know.

JAY. I was in…

JACOB. I know. I know. I read the paper.

(**JACOB** *exits,* **JAY** *sits.*)

JAY. Sarah, Glenlivet neat.

16

(Split scene. **FRANK** *King is on the phone at the National Desk. Elsewhere,* **JAY**, *in his apartment.* **JAY** *wears boxers.)*

*(***JAY***'s cell phone begins to ring, he stares at it in dread. It rings and rings...finally,* **JAY** *picks it up.)*

JAY. Times Bennett.

FRANK. Jay, it's Frank...

JAY. Frank?

FRANK. At National, I'm doing the lobster shift for Bob, the overnight... Sorry to call you so late.

JAY. Frank. Yeah. What's up?

FRANK. Good work on this sniper interrogation story. It just went on the website. It must be good because I'm getting calls from Federal Prosecutors at one in the morning...

JAY. What?

FRANK. DiBiagio just called. He's furious. I'm the only one here, I thought I should call. I need to leave the late note, I already gave the goodnight.

JAY. DiBiagio called?

FRANK. He was worked up, Jay...he...

JAY. What did he say?

FRANK. Well, you know, he says your story is, how does one say this? Is bullshit. Those where his words. Called it bullshit. Said that he never called and stopped the interrogation of the sniper by the local cops. Said that this John Muhammed wasn't about to confess...he was hot.

JAY. Typical. My sources say otherwise.

FRANK. He wanted to know who you talked to. He was livid.

JAY. What did you tell him?

FRANK. To go jump in a lake. This is The New York Times, we don't hand over sources…even when there are five unnamed ones in the story.

JAY. The sources are good.

FRANK. I know. I was just kidding.

JAY. The quotes are good. You know what these state versus federal pissing matches are like, nobody goes on the record… The local authorities were livid with having the feds come in and take the case…they only had seven hours with the guy, the Feds are measuring dicks.

FRANK. I know.

JAY. This is by the book.

FRANK. I just need to talk to you, for the late note. Also to warn you, this guy is going to be calling again in the morning, says he going to have another press conference to respond to your story specifically. Needless to say, you might be getting more phone calls. You might want to rehearse…

JAY. Rehearse? Frank.

FRANK. Relax, Jay. You just humiliated a Federal Prosecutor on the front page of The New York Times. This is to be expected. That being said, I wouldn't go asking his office for an interview anytime soon.

JAY. Noted.

FRANK. It wouldn't be good journalism if it didn't cause a shit storm.

JAY. I'm in Rockville now… I'm still trying to get these guys to go on the record. I'm working.

FRANK. Rockville, huh?

(**JAY** *opens his laptop, types a few key strokes.*)

JAY. Yeah. In my room at the Best Western on…1251 West Montgomery Avenue.

FRANK. How precise of you.

JAY. I'm looking out at the parking lot right now. I see… fourteen cars… It's an extended stay hotel, lots of journalists staying here… I was just at the hotel bar. It was a who's who…every paper east of the Mississippi. A real party, but I gotta work so… I don't know how those guys do it…

FRANK. Sounds about right. Do you like DC?

JAY. It's my hometown. So, no.

FRANK. I used to work there. I was a deputy, under Abe… back in the seventies. Worst two years of my life. A real one horse town… A big fat bureaucratic, cocktail party going horse.

JAY. You did live here.

FRANK. Well, that's the heads up. Expect a call in the morning. Don't take any shit.

JAY. Thanks for the call. Maybe I'll see you next time I'm in New York.

FRANK. I doubt it. I won't be here. They're retiring me.

JAY. Really? I'm sorry to hear that.

FRANK. I got another couple months. With advertising in the dumps since the attack, they already have a hiring freeze going on…and now they are strongly encouraging us oldies to take the buyout.

JAY. Congratulations. I guess? What should I say?

FRANK. I don't know what I'm going to do now.

JAY. Take it easy…you've earned it.

FRANK. It would be hard to take it much easier than I already do… I sit and read the wires, and every once in a while I get to make a phone call like this…and that, oh, that is really exciting. Then I write my little note and…but, at least, I feel like I'm part of something every once in awhile.

JAY. Part of something.

FRANK. It's nice to talk to someone. I'm just here in case the building catches on fire…I can pull the alarm. They had a monkey work this shift, but he died. At least I'll finally be able to finish my novel.

*(**FRANK** laughs. **JAY** smiles. The moment fades.)*
JAY. Thanks for the call.
FRANK. Yeah. Good work, Jay. Keep up the good work.
*(**FRANK** hangs up.)*

17

(A new image of a Mexican American woman sitting on a couch, she has a photo of her son, a soldier, in her lap.)

*(**MONICA** Soria, now a reporter in Texas, reads her story from her newspaper. Elsewhere **JAY** Bennett does the same with his story in the* Times.*)*

MONICA. Dateline San Antonio, April 18, Monica Soria, The San Antonio Express. "Words can hardly describe the emotions Rosa Arenas has experienced since learning her 24-year-old son was missing, 'somewhere in Iraq .' Rosa Arenas, 40, of Los Fresnos, sits in her daughter's room near an altar she has built for her son, Edward Arenas, 24, missing in action in Iraq since March 23."

(Another image of Rosa Arenas, she points at a ceiling fan, still clutching her son's photo.)

"So the single mother points to the ceiling fan he installed in her small living room. She points to the white couches, the tennis bracelet still in its red velvet case and the Martha Stewart patio furniture, all gifts from her first born and only son."

JAY. Dateline San Antonio, April 26, Jay Bennett, The New York Times. "Rosa Arenas points proudly to the white couches, the tennis bracelet in its red case and the Martha Stewart furniture out on the patio. She proudly points up to the ceiling fan, the lamp for Mother's Day, the entertainment center that arrived last Christmas and all the other gifts from her only son, Edward, a 24-year-old Army mechanic."

(Another photo projected, highlighting the identical quotes.)

*(**MONICA** and **JAY** speak in unison.)*

MONICA. "I wish I could talk to a mother who is in the same shoes as I am who has her son missing in action. It's very hard."

JAY. "I wish I could talk to a mother who is in the same shoes as I am who has her son missing in action. It's very hard."

MONICA. Said Arenas, who speaks haltingly.

JAY. Arenas said, her voice breaking.

MONICA. "Sleep these days only comes with a pill. She said she has moments when she can picture her son in some Iraqi village, like the ones she has seen on TV, surrounded by a herd of animals and the Iraqis he has befriended."

JAY. "At moments, Ms. Arenas says, she can picture her son in an Iraqi village, like the ones she has seen on television, surrounded by animals and the Iraqi people he has befriended. She said that while she still might have hope, sleep these days comes only in the form of a pill that the doctors gave her."

MONICA. "I'll sleep when my boy comes home. Where he belongs, here in my arms."

JAY. "I'll sleep when my boy comes home. Where he belongs, here in my arms."

(Another photo projected, highlighting the identical quotes. **MONICA** *Soria folds her paper and exits.* **JAY** *continues.)*

(A new projection of a run-down, Mexican American neighborhood in San Antonio. The image shows a small house with a dying tree in it's yard, a yellow ribbon tied around the tree.)

"In the Arenas' yard, a withered tree is wrapped in a yellow ribbon. A somber reminder of a missing son, and a neighborhood decimated by a far away war."

*(***JAY*** folds his paper and exits.)*

18

(HAL's office. HAL, JUNIOR and GERALD sip tumblers of Bourbon, a day done...)

HAL. ...It's like I told you, you have to change with the times. I mean that IS the NAME of the paper, isn't it? The New York TIMES? You can't expect to expand a brand to a new generation of readers when your prized art section only covers Austrian chamber music festivals and the latest Sotheby's auction. I put my foot in that section's ass, and people are talking about Arts and Leisure again, because Arts and Leisure is covering things that they actually, excuse my french, give a shit about.

JUNIOR. And I supported you then, as I do now.

HAL. I'm just saying, everywhere I look around here, I see dead weight...dead brush, that needs to be cleared. This is the only place in the world where you can never get fired.

JUNIOR. We've made inroads. The buyouts have been a success.

HAL. I need my people! I need my people leading the charge. Can I have your wallet?

JUNIOR. I'm sorry?

HAL. I want to take my wife out for dinner tonight. Give me your wallet.

JUNIOR. You want my wallet?

HAL. Come on, hand it over.

JUNIOR. Now, Hal...

HAL. Oh, so, you don't like to be stolen from? Well, that is news to me...stop the presses. Because everywhere I look I see people stealing money from you, Junior.

JUNIOR. You got me there...

HAL. But you get my point? Am I wrong here? Gerald?

GERALD. There needs to be restructuring, in my opinion. We have a war going on, the city is rebuilding…it is an important time. We need people we trust.

HAL. Trust is the word.

JUNIOR. I understand. But some of these people have worked here, loyally, for a very long time…plus, with the union…

HAL. The goddamn union. I loved it when I was a member, now I could care less.

JUNIOR. And, well, quite frankly, you can't just fire everybody…

HAL. Reassign them then. I'll create a new bureau in Antarctica, we'll send them there.

GERALD. The outer space bureau?

HAL. The wasted space bureau.

JUNIOR. I think some… I don't know…restraint should be used. We can't act like a bull in a china shop.

HAL. I'm not a bull, I'm a bear. I'm Bear Bryant. We won seven Pulitzers last year. Circulation is up. Nobody is talking about Wen Ho Lee anymore… Now, we have an opportunity to put our boot on the neck of the Washington Post, and squeeze the life out of them. But I need your support. You have to trust me.

JUNIOR. I do.

HAL. Well, let's drink to that. Hmm. That is good.

(They all toast.)

A long way from burgers on the steps in Washington, Gerald.

JUNIOR. What other changes do you have in mind?

GERALD. I think Metro needs a change.

JUNIOR. You want to replace Ben? But Metro…

GERALD. My two cents. I think his attitude gets in the way of his performance. Ducks in a line, right? Well, Ben is out of line.

HAL. I trust Gerald's judgment. Hell, he ran that section before Ben.

JUNIOR. I'll have to consider it.

HAL. I want an overhaul, Junior. I'll have a list of my recommendations on your desk in the morning.

(A phone rings. **HAL** *answers.)*

Yes? He is. Now? I'll tell him. You have a phone call. It's Kurtz over at the Washington Post.

GERALD. What's he want? Did Catherine talk to him? Okay. I'll take it in my office.

*(***GERALD*** goes to take his phone call.)*

HAL. Speak of the Devil and he shall appear.

JUNIOR. Kurtz at the Washington Post?

HAL. Media reporter. He takes every opportunity to bash us, probably found a double period on page A29 and wants a statement about why it occurred.

JUNIOR. We'll implement your plan, Hal. You have the publisher's blessing.

*(***HAL*** smiles and finishes his drink, as he does,* ***GERALD*** *enters, he is more serious now. He sits, saying nothing.)*

HAL. Well, what did ol' Howie Kurtz want?

GERALD. We have a problem.

19

(MONICA Soria's phone rings and rings, finally her Machine answers.)

MONICA. *(voice over)* "This is Monica Soria, please leave your reason for calling and your number."

(The machine's chime rings. There is a long silence. Then MONICA enters and answers. Silence.)

Hello? *(beat)* Jacob? *(beat)* Who is this? *(beat)* Jay? Why are you calling here?

Yes, there's *a very simple one.*

All you did was rearrange the story.

I thought so, that's why I don't understand this. What? Are you serious?

That's good, Jay. But, it has nothing to do with... There is no *we*, Jay.

So you can take whatever you want...my words, this woman's life...

No. You don't know what it feels like to be...

*You took my voice...*the one that couldn't even get me... I started in community college and got to the newsroom of The New York Times...but you got it. You got the job...and what do you do with it? A friend, I thought... It hurts so bad...so...I'm getting off the phone now.

(silence)

You wanna talk about the facts, Jay?

The furniture was still in it's box in the garage. In the article...*your version...*

you say the "Martha Stewart furniture out on the patio." The furniture, like the tennis bracelet...were both in the original boxes. They weren't out, or displayed... A mother with a missing son halfway around the world doesn't have the energy or interest to assemble patio furniture by herself. To be proud of it? I called her... they're still in the boxes. That's the facts, Jay.

You weren't there. You never went to her house, did you? You were never there, Jay.
The furniture was still in the boxes. You were never there. You were never there.

20

*(**GERALD**'s office. **GERALD** sits across from **JAY**. A short silence.)*

GERALD. Jay.

JAY. I've talked to Jim about this...and...

GERALD. Jay, I've been on the phone with Robert Rivard, the executive editor of the San Antonio Express. He called, seeing if I wanted to thank him.

JAY. For what?

GERALD. He wanted me to thank him for having his reporter write a story for The New York Times.

JAY. I told Jim what must have happened.

GERALD. Howard Kurtz is running a story in tomorrow's Washington Post detailing the similarities between your story and Monica's. This is serious, Jay.

JAY. I understand that... Her story got mixed in with my notes. I must've...I must've...

GERALD. This is serious, Jay.

JAY. I know... There are cases where this has happened before, I looked it up... This Baltimore Sun columnist...

GERALD. Jay, you know we protect our reporters.

JAY. Well, I don't feel protected right now.

GERALD. But we need your cooperation.

JAY. Cooperation? I told you, her story...my notes... I just...

GERALD. We need proof that you where in Los Fresnos.

JAY. What? Of course I was. What is this?

GERALD. We need receipts. The hotel, the rental car...

JAY. Okay. Okay. My credit cards are maxed and I had to sleep in my car. It's embarrassing. I told Jim about the rental car, ask him.

GERALD. They don't have you on record as renting a car.

JAY. Then I told you the wrong place. I'll go and I'll get them.

GERALD. Sit down.

JAY. Let me just go home and review the… I was there, Gerald. This is starting to piss me off.

GERALD. The family, this mother Rosa Arenas, doesn't remember talking to you. She's talked to a lot of press, but she doesn't remember someone from the Times.

JAY. She's wrong.

GERALD. Jay. Listen to me. This is the situation. This is happening, brother. If you want us to protect you, we need proof. Hard evidence. People are saying…

JAY. What? I didn't do anything wrong.

GERALD. Something is amiss, Jay.

JAY. Are you going to suspend me?

GERALD. You're gonna be suspended at a minimum, Jay. I don't think you're listening.

JAY. I am.

GERALD. Then talk to me. Tell me the truth.

JAY. The truth is… I work for The New York Times, I'm a writer for The New York Times. I'm a newspaper writer, Gerald. It's in my blood…it's…who I am. So, to insinuate…it's offensive. I have done everything this place has asked me to do…and maybe it has eaten me up a little…maybe I've given too much…I need a little rest. I've been around these families, these families that have been blown up by the war…crying mothers and fathers, who, when you look into their eyes you see no light, just this absence of…anything, like dark empty rooms. I have to look into their eyes and say, "what does it feel like?" What does it feel like to have your son or daughter die this terrible way, and "who do you blame?" And please don't take too long to articulate it, because I have a seven-thirty deadline, and then I have to file my expenses…plus I gotta get out of town tomorrow to talk to another family, push my way into their living room, and ask them the same goddamn questions.

GERALD. I understand the pressure. But that is the job.

JAY. All I ever wanted to do was write for this paper, my whole life…and it happened. Do you know what that feels like? To be hurt by something you love. To hurt something you… Do you understand? *(beat)* Now you? Not you. To be scorned. I love this place…it's my home.

GERALD. I do understand. I've given my entire adult life to this paper…my first marriage, a woman I loved very much, I gave her up for this place. I understand, Jay. See? But you have to understand, that if you love this place you have to tell me how deep this goes. It's not just a newspaper, Jay. It's a symbol, and idea… It's the truth… It is a public trust…and once that trust is shattered, it will never come back, unless we're totally forthright about what happened. Help me. Please, Jay…

JAY. What do you want to hear? Yes. I made mistakes.

GERALD. Mistakes?

JAY. Yes.

GERALD. Plural. More than one? Are there others? How many?

JAY. I don't know. Mistakes were made.

GERALD. How many mistakes, Jay? Is this isolated? This looks bad. You don't have a lot of friends around here right now. Just help us sort this out. Is this a one time thing? Jay, are you listening? Look at me…is it?

JAY. One time thing? We're friends, right? Still?

GERALD. This is an office, and I am your superior. I care about you, like I care about all these people who I work with.

JAY. I was special though. I wrote about you, I nominated you for that award, I bragged about you. WE HAVE HISTORY.

GERALD. I never asked for any of that.

JAY. But, I did anyway. So, you'd like me..so you'd… Fuck. What did they tell you?

GERALD. I'm sorry?

JAY. Go get that runaway slave. Bring him home. Is that what they said? Gerald, you're black, reel that nigger in…brother to brother.

GERALD. No.

JAY. Then why aren't I in Hal's office? Tell me that. Why aren't I in Junior's office? Why am I in your office, Gerald?

GERALD. I'm the managing editor.

JAY. Who's kidding who?

GERALD. You wanna talk brother to brother? Do you realize what this could mean? Brother to brother. What it'll mean for…

JAY. Come on, Uganda X…

GERALD. We have to be better. You never understood that, or I didn't make it clear. This. Whatever it is…will destroy everything we have worked for…everything… It'll bring us all down.

JAY. You know what they call you and Hal? Huck Finn and Nigger Jim.

GERALD. Race - me and you, what we are - shouldn't have anything to do with this.

JAY. But it will. Isn't that the story? What's the story, Gerald? If you were writing it…what would you lede with?

GERALD. You tell me.

JAY. A young New York Times reporter… No. A brilliant young New York Times reporter…

GERALD. You're burying your lede.

JAY. A brilliant young New York Times reporter…made a mistake…he…he… Stop. Don't you see what these people are trying to do? Trying to divide us. Father versus son.

GERALD. I'm not your father, Jay…

JAY. He died in Vietnam.

GERALD. I thought he worked for the Pentagon?

JAY. Yeah. I mean, no. Should I get a lawyer?

GERALD. No. The truth. Tell me!

JAY. Don't yell at me!

GERALD. I'm sorry. The cardinal rule, Jay. Did you fabricate, did you steal? Tell me…tell me. It'll be all right. I promise. But we have to start with the truth.

JAY. It'll be alright? You promise? I'll still have a job, no matter what?

GERALD. Jay, I can't promise that.

JAY. Promise.

GERALD. I can't do that, Jay. You know that.

JAY. Promise me, you'll still be my friend.

GERALD. I'm still your friend. But that means you're my friend…my friends tell me their secrets.

JAY. You said you'd be watching me. I wanted you to be proud of me.

GERALD. Maybe I did look at you and see something familiar. A distant…

JAY. What?

GERALD. I'm guilty of that. God knows. I don't know how I'm going to live with… But now is not the time to dwell… We'll go through every story you ever wrote, Jay. We'll find out. It'll all be there…in black and white. Just make it easier.

JAY. You're right. You're not my father. You're my Uncle Tom.

GERALD. Jay.

JAY. I'll resign, then you won't be able to make me do anything. I'll write a book. A book about this place. I know where all the bodies are buried.

GERALD. No. We are going to sit here and figure this out.

JAY. This interview is over. You'll have my resignation shortly.

GERALD. Jay. Don't do this.

JAY. It is going to make a great story, Gerald. It is going to make a *great* story.

(**JAY** *exits.*)

22

*(Split scene. **HAL**'s office.)*

*(**HAL** and **GERALD** wait anxiously, they are preparing to attend an employee talkback concerning the **JAY** Bennett scandal.)*

*(Elsewhere, somewhere outside this office, **JUNIOR**, a bag in his hand, speaks to **BEN**.)*

BEN. You're asking my opinion?

JUNIOR. A trusted voice. With a…great future ahead of you. I have decisions to make, and I… *(beat)* I'm trying to gauge the troops' morale.

BEN. The troops? I can't speak for the troops, but the staff, the newsroom, feels…angry. Betrayed. Embarrassed. Furious, really.

JUNIOR. At me?

(Silence. A look.)

BEN. Ask your winners. *(beat)* I'm sure you'll make it right, Junior, that you'll do the *right thing*.

*(**BEN** thrusts his hand out toward **JUNIOR**, who takes it and shakes it. **BEN** exits.)*

*(**GERALD** stares at them, **HAL** opines while looking at the other papers.)*

HAL. "The *Jay Bennett* Scandal." "The Jay Bennett *Scandal.*" It does have a ring to it, doesn't it? I wish I'd thought of it myself. Kinda rolls off the tongue…like Watergate or the Iran-Contra Affair. "The Jay Bennett Affair," is too vague. "Jay Bennett, lone plagiarist," is too accurate. Scandal says it all. A conspiracy. *(beat)* We should never be the story. The country is still at war…Caligula is in the White House and all anybody can talk about is us. These fucking bloggers…not a goddamned journalist among them, but it doesn't matter…just a laptop and boatload of opinions…they're going to bury us all. Sometimes I just want to shake the whole damn world till it shuts up and listens. When we first met, all those years ago in Washington, did you ever imagine we'd be here…sitting right here like this, Gerald? Gerald?

GERALD. *(distracted)* Hm? Sorry. What do you think they are talking about?

HAL. Who?

GERALD. Junior and Ben.

HAL. I'm not sure, but I suspect it has to do with our little situation.

GERALD. Do you think…? Look at them, smiling, nodding… Junior kissing his ass. Ben has a job for life…

HAL. It'll drive you crazy, if you think about it too much, my friend.

GERALD. Why are you so calm?

HAL. Bourbon.

(**JUNIOR** *and* **BEN** *finish up their silent talk.* **JUNIOR** *heads toward* **HAL**'s *office.* **GERALD** *and* **BEN** *lock eyes, something is communicated.* **JUNIOR** *enters, placing his bag down.*)

JUNIOR. How is my team holding up?

HAL. I feel like Nixon during the last days. "I am not a crook."

JUNIOR. It's for the troops, Hal, nothing to worry about. Just a friendly talkback with the staff.

GERALD. I can smell the burning torches from here.

JUNIOR. Transparency, Gerald. It's our responsibility to be as open to our staff as humanly possible. Start an honest dialogue about where mistakes were made, and then move on.

(**JUNIOR** *removes a large stuffed animal from the bag he was carrying, he places it on* **HAL**'s *desk. They all take it in.*)

HAL. Can I ask you something, Junior? What in the hell is that?

JUNIOR. It is a mnemonic device, a reminder and symbol of the issues that concern everybody but that they were afraid to discuss. It is call for honesty.

HAL. Jesus, Junior, it's a stuffed animal. You want us to stand out in front of these people who work *for* us, on our knees, with only a goddamned stuffed animal to protect us? I need a refill.

JUNIOR. It's a mnemonic device, they're very useful in these situations. I took a seminar…

HAL. Well, I'll be sure to remember that, when I refer all my questions to Paddington Bear over here.

(**JUNIOR** *drops some note cards,* **GERALD** *glances at them.*)

GERALD. Are we going to review these?

JUNIOR. They're questions that Catherine in public relations has drawn up, things the staff may ask during the town hall. Just so we are all on the same page. Shall we look at them?

HAL. Oh Christ, must we? I mean, I think I can handle myself quite fine without being overly rehearsed.

GERALD. The whole thing is a bad idea.

JUNIOR. Gerald, I need you to get on board.

GERALD. Easy for you to say, you weren't blamed for another man's deceit in your own newspaper.

JUNIOR. You weren't blamed. The article had plenty of blame for everybody, let's not wallow.

GERALD. Is that how you read it? It was a bad idea to have that article, that soon. Five years of deceit and lying by that… *Five years* and our reporters had *four days* to dig through all the lies, then *three days* of silence from the masthead…

HAL. I stand by the article, Gerald. As much as it hurts… I stand by it. Did it turn out the way I wanted? No. Hell no. But the only way to combat bad journalism is with good journalism. They did good work.

GERALD. Thirty-six. Thirty-six articles with fabrications. God knows how many more?

HAL. Sonofabitch didn't even graduate from college. How do we not check these things?

GERALD. Fooled us all. The staff is embarrassed…they had to blame somebody. Now this dog and pony show…

JUNIOR. You'll excuse me, if I want to take care to protect the legacy of this newspaper and my family… You'll be *so good* as to grant me that *small* favor.

GERALD. I'm sorry. I have another headache. It's all very fresh.

JUNIOR. We have to present a united front. We have to not be on the defensive, but rather listen to their thoughts and complaints. You are my team. Hal? Okay then, after Hal and I give our opening remarks…

GERALD. Do I not get some time? I'd like to defend myself. I was called Jay's protector on the McNeil-Lehrer News Hour last night…

JUNIOR. You'll have time to speak, but first I'll say a few words, then Hal, then we'll open up the floor to questions. Now lets see… Remember, LISTEN DON'T DEFEND. Gerald ask one.

(**GERALD** *takes a card from the pile.*)

GERALD. What steps as Publisher are you planning on taking to avoid another scandal such as this?

JUNIOR. Well, first off, I.. Well, we'll, ah, assemble a committee of our top editors. Ah…

HAL. *(clapping)* Bravo. Perhaps you should have the stuffed animal answer after all.

(**JUNIOR**, *humbled, takes a card.*)

JUNIOR. Hal, why did Jay receive a second chance at the Times?

HAL. Well, that is good question. I can only say I was raised in the segregated south and it was a painful experience to live through, and something that deeply affected my views on race and opportunity. Perhaps it was this experience that shaded my response to Jay's troubles, perhaps it was watching young men of color time and time again be denied a chance, much less, what I was raised to see as the God given right of a second chance... Unfortunately, as we all know, this was a mistake and I regret giving Jay that chance. But it will not, in the future, keep me from seeing the best in my troops.

GERALD. It sounds like a campaign speech. Four more years.

HAL. It is.

JUNIOR. I like it, I like the personal anecdote. It's humanizing.

GERALD. Honestly, I found it patronizing. I think members of the staff might feel the same way. I think we should avoid race. This is not the failure of a minority journalist that reflects on other minority journalists... let's not make this about race or youth. This was an isolated, fucked-up kid.

HAL. It's my truth, it's how I feel. I think the truth is our best weapon.

GERALD. Should we take hands and sing, "We Shall Overcome?"

HAL. I'm glad you find this funny.

GERALD. Here is a question for you, Hal. *Some* have charged that your leadership style is arrogant, isolated and autocratic...do you think these traits help foster the environment that allowed Jay Bennett to succeed at deceiving the entire New York Times for years?

HAL. That is a leading question, one I find offensive...

GERALD. We are about to enter a theater full of the best reporters and editors in the world, you don't think they're going to ask follow up questions? Ask better questions than Catherine from PR can dream up? I'm doing you a favor.

HAL. I have run this newspaper the only way I know how, with balls. I didn't hear anybody complaining before this happened…

GERALD. Of course you didn't hear them. You were in your office playing with your balls, I was out in the newsroom doing your bidding…

HAL. You ungrateful sonofa…

GERALD. Listen, don't defend, Hal.

HAL. Then a question for you. Why didn't you tell the National desk about Jay's past problems when you moved him there?

GERALD. It was a mistake. One I regret.

HAL. Didn't you encourage his hiring over other candidates?

GERALD. As did you… At the time he was a very productive reporter.

HAL. A very productive *black* reporter.

JUNIOR. Gentlemen.

GERALD. Yes. A very productive black reporter. But that…

HAL. Isn't this just affirmative action run amuck? A personal, race based agenda?

GERALD. No! Hal. I did what I thought was best, what I was hired to do, at all times. I.

HAL. I'm sorry, Gerald. But I was once a hell of a reporter too. I was just helping you out, like you said.

GERALD. Is that why you picked me?

HAL. What?

GERALD. Is that why you picked me as Managing Editor? Out of some white Southerner guilt?

HAL. Jesus, Gerald.

GERALD. Come on…was I some social experiment? I never thought of myself as a token…never once…

HAL. No.

GERALD. Just another saccharine sweet parable from you? "Lessons from Hal."

HAL. You are ten pounds of shit in a five pound bag, right now...

GERALD. Or...was I just the scary nig...

JUNIOR. Stop. Stop, both of you. This has to stop.

(Silence. Deep breaths.)

When my father was Publisher, he pushed the coverage of the civil rights movement, he integrated the newsroom...he felt it was his responsibility to make the paper reflect the country. He felt a kinship with African Americans and their struggle...because he was a Jew and had faced discrimination and despised it... He wanted the paper to be a weapon against it...to shine the light of truth on these disgusting things. He wanted the paper to show the way, from the inside out. I won't stand for this ugliness, not here.

HAL. History is going to judge us, and there is very little we can do about it. But, perhaps, we can clarify a few things along the way. We're all in this together after all, for better or worse.

GERALD. For better or worse.

JUNIOR. Well, I'm sure we'll be fine. Just fine. We should get ready to head over there.

HAL. Yep...time to piss on the fire and call the dogs.

*(The three men, various degrees of defeated, straighten themselves up. As they get ready to go. **HAL**, fingers the cards.)*

Oh, there is one more question here for Junior.

JUNIOR. We should really be going.

HAL. As publisher will you be seeking the resignations of your executive editor and managing editor?

JUNIOR. Is that really written there?

HAL. Answer the question.

(A moment passes. A unconscious beat, a liar's breath...a tell.)

JUNIOR. No. I won't, and I won't accept them if offered.

*(**HAL**, **GERALD** and **JUNIOR** exit, a solemn retreat. A moment passes and **JUNIOR** returns, having forgotten his stuffed animal. He looks at the toy.)*

How did we end up here?

*(**JUNIOR** goes to the door, takes a breath, and exits.)*

22

(Park Slope, Brooklyn. **JACOB** *moves suitcases full of stuff from an unseen apartment. He is overloaded.)*

(A moment passes, and **JAY** *walks up. They can't avoid one another, although* **JAY** *tries to…it is hopeless.)*

JACOB. Jay? Jay!

JAY. I didn't see you.

JACOB. Really?

JAY. I don't know.

JACOB. Well, this is…awkward. I thought I should call out to you…now I don't know why I did.

JAY. Yeah. I haven't seen anybody from the paper.

JACOB. I imagine not.

JAY. It wasn't as bad as you might think. There were some kind people. Understanding.

JACOB. Nothing surprises me anymore. I, ah…I don't know what to say.

JAY. Me neither. Any good gossip?

JACOB. Yeah, this brilliant kid pissed away his career making up stories.

JAY. I heard that. I should be going.

JACOB. Oh. Frank King killed himself.

JAY. What?

JACOB. Yeah. On his retirement day. Dove out of the 12th floor smokers window.

JAY. No shit?

JACOB. Had a note pinned to him, just said "Timesman."

JAY. Jesus Christ. That makes me…so sad.

JACOB. I often imagined punching you, or something…

JAY. I'm sorry. We were friends.

JACOB. Exactly. I have to ask. Monica? Why? You stole from Monica?

JAY. It wasn't personal. I needed to destroy myself and that was the easiest way.

JACOB. I read that quote in The Observer and The New Yorker and The Sun. Been quite a publicity tour, hasn't it?

JAY. I guess.

JACOB. You... It was all a game? Wasn't it? An act...no, a party trick, right?

JAY. No.

JACOB. Jay Bennett, born in Washington D.C. Mother, Maureen, is a secretary at Georgetown University. Father, Lloyd, lives in Ohio with his second wife and has for fifteen years, he is not close with his son. A gifted...I mean that...a gifted journalist...Jay was the editor of the school newspaper at Maryland University, before accepting an exclusive internship at The New York Times. You lied to everybody, even your friends...

JAY. I was sick.

JACOB. Fuck you, Jay, seriously. You pusillanimous...

JAY. Bi-polar disorder, they think...I've been seeing doctors...

JACOB. Oh yeah, you're mentally ill... Or are you a drunk cokehead? Which is it? I can't keep up. Or maybe, just maybe...you're full of shit. I used to think you were Nick Carraway, but it was an act...you were Gatsby...a phoney, a fake.

JAY. I love that...I'm a fake and pariah, but Stephen Glass who did the same thing at The New Republic is a white wunderkind who cleverly deceived his editors. I'm a criminal, he's a prankster.

JACOB. I'm sorry you didn't receive better reviews as a plagiarist, Jay, really.

JAY. Look how it's been covered, tell me there isn't a difference...

JACOB. Race? You must know what you've done for your race, Jay. It must have crossed your mind that every other black kid who wants to be a journalist will be judged differently because of you...what you did. You are a testament, really.

JAY. I didn't mean to hurt anybody but myself.

JACOB. Well, you failed at that, Jay...you hurt a lot of people. Monica. Hal was an asshole, but he didn't deserve to lose his job over you, neither did Gerald, your good buddy... Me. You hurt me.

JAY. I lost my career, Jacob.

JACOB. Lost? You threw it away. Don't worry, I'm sure the race- baiting book you're hawking will make you rich. Trash the one thing in the world you cared most about, AFTER damaging it beyond repair. If you can't trust a newspaper, it becomes useless. Do you understand that? Every time we publish a story about some terrible wrong in the world or government abuse they're going to say, "Who knows if it's even true? Look at what Jay Bennett did."

JAY. True? Say what you want, but my stories where always true, I gave the truth...but not the...

JACOB. The what? The facts?

JAY. If you can't understand the difference, then who's the fool?

(**JACOB** *looks on in amazement.*)

JACOB. Well, you achieved one of your goals. They're going to teach about you in journalism classes...you're famous, Jay. You're assured of getting your obituary in the Times.

JAY. Great. You can write it.

JACOB. I don't think so.

JAY. Why not? In fact, I'm asking you to.

JACOB. I'm going to Iraq. This stuff goes into storage, immersion courses, then...I'm off.

JAY. Foreign. You got transferred to the Foreign Desk?

JACOB. War correspondent.

JAY. Wow. I. Congratulations, Jacob. I don't think there is much else to…I should go.

JACOB. Wait. Can I ask you something? Why? Why did you do it?

JAY. Always the reporter.

JACOB. Someone has to be.

JAY. I thought I told you.

JACOB. There is always an extra question to ask.

JAY. There is never an easy answer. On the record or off?

JACOB. On. Off. I don't care. Tell me.

JAY. I… You'll have to buy the book.

(Silence. He turns and walks away slowly from **JACOB**.*)*

24

(**HAL** *enters.*)

HAL. Sleep did not come easy last night, but when it did, I dreamt. It was unlike any dream I could remember, it felt ancient and far reaching, with people from my past and others I didn't know… In it, my first wife is there and she said to me sweetly, that's how I knew it was a dream, "you're just looking for an excuse to go fishing," and I turned to her and said, "I don't need one now." You never know when you are going to wake up to a story…in a story. *(beat)* This profession, this calling…has been my life's work, a life…and before I shuffle off to the world of dry flies and fiction…I have no great wisdom to impart, and even if I did, I don't know if you'd want to hear it…but I can offer you this: When the next great story breaks, you'll know it…and when you know it…you go like hell.

(Behind **HAL** *the world sizzles and fades to a black out)*

End of play

www.ingramcontent.com/pod-product-compliance
Lightning Source LLC
Chambersburg PA
CBHW071411290426
44108CB00014B/1776